Gifts We Bring To Honor The King

Sermons And Worship Resources
For Advent And Christmas

David M. Oliver

CSS Publishing Company, Inc., Lima, Ohio

GIFTS WE BRING TO HONOR THE KING

Library of Congress Cataloging-in-Publication Data

Oliver, David M.
Gifts we bring to honor the king : sermon and worship resources for Advent/Christmas / David M. Oliver.
p. cm.
ISBN 0-7880-1124-3 (pbk.)
1. Advent. 2. Christmas. 3. Worship programs. 4. Advent sermons. 5. Christmas sermons. I. Title.
BV40.045 1997
264—dc21 97-15983
CIP

This book is available in the following formats, listed by ISBN:
0-7880-1124-3 Book
0-7880-1125-1 Mac
0-7880-1126-X IBM 3 1/2
0-7880-1127-8 Sermon Prep

PRINTED IN U.S.A.

This book is dedicated to the members and friends of Smithville United Methodist Church who have enriched my life immeasurably with their prayers, encouragement, and clear evidence of Christian discipleship.

Acknowledgments

I am grateful to my mentors, Jim and Phyllis Lange, who helped me to answer God's call to ministry and who shared the initial idea of having congregation members bring something to church each Sunday during Advent. My appreciation is extended to Priscilla Gresser for her advice in selecting the wide variety of music which is suggested for each of the Sundays.

I have been richly blessed by my parents, Leon and Helen Oliver, whose love for God and one another has been an inspiration and a source of sustenance. Special heartfelt thanks goes to my wife Jane Hoyt-Oliver, and our daughter Michelle, for being my primary companions in love and on the spiritual journey. Each of you has given me great joy and stability in the sometimes rocky road of faith.

May the living Lord continue to aid us in loving one another and growing in our life together. For all that has been ... thanks. For all that will be ... hallelujah!

David M. Oliver
Eastertide, 1997

Table Of Contents

Preface

This Advent/Christmas series is different. Instead of the congregation being passive observers of the drama of worship, they are involved weekly. By asking people to bring simple items or, in some cases, certain attitudes, church members are included in creating meaningful worship for God, who is the true audience and recipient of our common worship life.

On the first Sunday in Advent people bring bells to announce Christ's coming. Lighting candles as a reminder that Christ is the light of the world, and so are we, is the focus of the second Sunday in Advent. Presenting a special gift or sum of money for a mission project reminds us, on the third Sunday in Advent, that Jesus Christ is God's gift to us and we are to be God's gift to the world. On the fourth Sunday in Advent, people are invited to bring a special measure of joy. God's Son is to be awaited and greeted with joy in a world desperately needing something solid on which to build a life of meaning and significance.

Christmas Eve/Day focuses on the theme of coming to Bethlehem with the attitude of awe and expectation. This is the place that God chose heaven and earth to meet. People are invited to look for God in this present moment.

On the first Sunday after Christmas, we contemplate what it means to be ever-green Christians, exploring how to be steadily fruitful and joyful in our walk of faith. People are to bring a cutting of an evergreen branch.

The second Sunday after Christmas is devoted to recommitting to Christ the gifts of our time, talents, and treasure. At the threshold of a new year, individuals are given the opportunity to make new commitments to God in the use of their gifts.

The fruit of this series in my local church was a more meaningful awareness among church members that they were responsible for preparing and bringing their weekly worship to God. They were not the audience. God was. As a result, they were true participants in the liturgy, which means "the work of the people." May this be so for you and your congregation as well.

Grace and Peace,
David M. Oliver

Music Sources

The hymns and choruses which are suggested in the worship service outlines are probably familiar to most congregations. A conscious attempt has been made to blend the traditional with the contemporary so that a variety of needs will be met in music.

The three sources cited below will give the people in charge of music the information they need to secure the songs for use in worship:

1. *Maranatha! Music Praise Chorus Book, Expanded 3rd Edition.* Nashville, TN: Word, Inc., 1993.

2. *The United Methodist Hymnal: Book of United Methodist Worship.* Nashville, TN: The United Methodist Publishing House, 1989.

3. *Worship His Majesty.* Alexandria, IN: Gaither Music Company, Inc., 1987.

First Sunday In Advent

Introduction to this Service:

Everyone is to come to church with some kind of **bell.** You will want to announce this the week prior and remind the congregation through other church communications. The following might be used in the newsletter or bulletin: "Bells have been used in many ways over the years. Bells have been used to sound an alarm, and to call children to school, people to worship, and families to meals. Bells mark the beginning and the end of the work day, classes, and sporting events. Sometimes bells mark the passing of the hours in a day. On this first Sunday of Advent, please bring a bell with you. We will be using the bells to call one another to a time of Advent waiting that is filled with anticipation."

The bells we ring will serve to help people to remember to wait with confident hope in Christ, even when it is difficult. Ringing the bells is a way of calling people to holy waiting in the context of a season which tempts us to give up waiting and entices us with myriad activities that ultimately will not strengthen but only frustrate and drain us.

CELEBRATING THE LORD'S DAY
FIRST SUNDAY IN ADVENT

OPENING SENTENCE 1 Corinthians 1:3

"Grace to you and peace from God our Father and the Lord Jesus Christ who was and is and is to come. Amen."

PRELUDE "God Rest You Merry, Gentlemen"
Trad. English Carol, arr. L. Smith

PARISH ANNOUNCEMENTS

*WELCOMING ONE ANOTHER

Shake hands with those around you. Introduce yourself to those you do not know by name. Please remain standing for the "Gathering."

*GATHERING "Adoration"
Randy Vader

*ADVENT WREATH CANDLE LIGHTING CEREMONY

Leader: "Take heed, watch; for you do not know when the time will come." (Mark 13:33)

People: We watch and wait in anticipation for the coming of the Christ Child. We prepare our hearts and minds for his coming. We submit our lives to the transforming power of his continued return.

Leader: The first candle in the Advent wreath represents our anticipation of Christ's coming. *(Light one candle.)* We ring the bells as we prepare for and announce the Coming One. We proclaim that he came, he is coming, and he will come again. Amen. *(Everyone rings their bells.)*

HYMN "O Come, O Come, Emmanuel"

CHILDREN'S MESSAGE

GIVING OF TITHES AND OFFERING

OFFERTORY ANTHEM "Angels We Have Heard on High"
Trad. French Carol, arr. L. Smith

PRAYER OF CONFESSION

Gracious and forgiving God, in this Advent Season we are called upon to set aside time to worship you and make new commitments. We need to take time to turn from our sin, reflect on your gifts to us, and consider how we might best dedicate ourselves to you once again. Forgive us for being consumed with other agenda that pushes you to the margins of our lives. As we announce your coming with the ringing of bells, help us also to prepare for your coming by waiting upon you and listening for you with eagerness and joy. Make this season truly holy for us. We pray these things in the name of Jesus Christ. Amen.

PRAYER SONG "Emmanuel, Emmanuel"

MORNING PRAYER and LORD'S PRAYER

ANTHEM "Soon and Very Soon"

OLD TESTAMENT LESSON Isaiah 64:1-9

Leader: This is the Word of the Lord.
People: Thanks be to God. Amen.

*GOSPEL LESSON Matthew 1:18-25

Leader: This is the Gospel of our Lord.
People: Praise be to you, Lord Jesus Christ. Amen.

*HYMN "Ring the Bells"

MORNING MESSAGE "Waiting With Anticipation"

HOLY COMMUNION

*HYMN "Let All Mortal Flesh Keep Silence"

*BLESSING

Leader: Go forth to actively wait upon the Lord. May Jesus Christ work in you this week to prepare you through waiting to be ready to announce his coming.

People: As we ring the bells, we joyfully anticipate what Christ will do in us and through us. Amen. *(Everyone rings their bells.)*

*BLESSING ONE ANOTHER and POSTLUDE

*All who are able please stand

Isaiah 64:1-9; Matthew 1:18-25

Waiting With Anticipation

Bells have been used in many ways over the years. Bells have been used to sound an alarm, and to call children to school, people to worship, and families to meals. Bells mark the beginning and end of the work day, classes, and sporting events. Sometimes bells mark the passing of the hours in a day. On this first Sunday of Advent we will be using the bells we have brought to call us to a time of waiting that is filled with anticipation.

The Old Testament lesson for this first Sunday of Advent looks forward to the time when God will intervene and reassert the divine reign on behalf of Judah. This announcement is greeted with anticipation and eagerness by some, with fear and trepidation by others.

The prophet Isaiah makes this contrast quite plain. In the midst of the nation's struggle, being exiled from their homeland and thus, the Hebrews believed, from God, Isaiah prays:

> *O that you would tear open the heavens and come down, so that the mountains would quake at your presence ... to make your name known to your adversaries, so that the nations might tremble at your presence! ... From ages past no one has heard, no ear has perceived, no eye has seen any God besides you, who works for those who wait for him. You meet those who gladly do right, those who remember you in your ways.*
>
> (Isaiah 64:1-5)

The prophet communicates deep, abiding faith in God during a time of uncertainty and travail. He looks to the One who can deliver the people from their oppression. He calls upon God to be their Advocate and intervene against their enemies to bring an end to their misery.

The profound realization of how far the people and nation have strayed is also underscored by the prophet's prayer:

> *But you were angry, and we sinned; because you hid yourself we transgressed. We have all become like one who is unclean, and all our righteous deeds are like a filthy cloth. We all fade like a leaf, and our iniquities, like the wind, take us away. There is no one who calls on your name ... for you have hidden your face from us, and have delivered us into the hand of our iniquity. Yet, O Lord, you are our Father; we are the clay, and you are our potter ... Do not be exceedingly angry, O Lord, and do not remember iniquity forever. Now consider, we are all your people.*
>
> (Isaiah 64:5-9)

Isaiah felt deeply the spiritual crisis of his people. He interceded before God on their behalf. He knew that God was their only hope. Despite the people's sin and separation, Isaiah boldly called on God. He acknowledged the plight of the nation and the people's need for divine intervention.

Isaiah's intercession offers a poignant contrast between God's power and the bondage of the people. He reveals in his prayer that the way to access divine power is through honest self-examination and confession. In this manner, the coming of the Lord can be greeted with anticipation and eagerness rather than with fear and trepidation.

Only when the people of God can look honestly at themselves do they discover the freedom and power to change. Lack of honesty, prideful self-justification, and attempting to lay blame on others creates barriers rather than removing them.

How can people of faith today gain this clarity and self-awareness? Isaiah offers us a direction with the following words: "... no eye has seen any God besides you, who works for those who **wait** for him" (Isaiah 64:4, emphasis added). The Hebrew word for "waiting" implies an active waiting rather than a passive waiting. This type of waiting is eager, expectant waiting. Biblical waiting involves steadfast, patient, faithful endurance. Waiting like this gives us the image of being on the edge of our seats, leaning forward, looking with keen interest toward God's next move. We might call this "full-alert" waiting. Waiting involves all our senses, all that we have, and all that we are, our whole being. The goal is to recognize and be responsive to the will of God and the Word of God. The feeling is hopeful. The focus is on God being our Helper, Deliverer, and Guide. **Let us sound our bells as a reminder to wait in this manner.** *(Pastor and people ring their bells.)*

"When God arrives on the scene with redemptive power, the response of those who have waited will be jubilant joy and great singing (Isaiah 25:9)."[1] Those who wait in this manner are blessed and energized by God. In another passage, Isaiah communicated the blessing and energy God gives to those who wait:

> *(God) does not faint or grow weary; his understanding is unsearchable. He gives power to the faint, and strengthens the powerless. Even youths will faint and be weary, and the young will fall exhausted; but those who* ***wait*** *for the Lord shall renew their strength, they shall mount up with wings like eagles, they shall run and not be weary, they shall walk and not faint.*
>
> (Isaiah 40:28-31, emphasis added).

Most of us would love to be renewed. The problem is that we find waiting difficult. We live in an "instant" society. We are used to things such as instant potatoes, instant hot cereal, instant coffee, instant global communication, and overnight package delivery anywhere in the world. We are aware of the dangers of instant gratification and impulse buying but, nevertheless, we are sometimes torn between resisting these things and embracing them. We are often quick to rationalize our actions and slow to assess carefully the implications of our actions. Many pitfalls await us on the road to renewal.

Advent is a good time to begin again this journey to renewal. On this first Sunday of Advent, we find ourselves at the start of a new season and the beginning of the Christian year. The word "advent" comes from a Latin word meaning "to come." Advent is a time of waiting and anticipation. But the waiting is difficult, even painful for us. Just ask a child what he or she thinks about waiting until Christmas. At times, waiting can feel like it will take forever! Nevertheless, the value of waiting is immeasurable.

I am convinced that we can only wait with persistent, confident, faithful hope when we are assured that there is purpose in our waiting. When we see waiting in light of a greater purpose of God, when we see waiting as a means of grace and as a means of growth, then we can learn to wait with greater patience. **Let us ring our bells to remember to wait in confident hope.** *(Pastor and people ring their bells.)*

The startling announcement of God's plan to Mary that she would have a child was heralded by an angel. This grand announcement, nevertheless, still involved waiting. *God* waited for Mary to accept the divine plan (Luke 1:38). *Mary* waited for the plan to be completed. The waiting also involved some tense times for Joseph and Mary, as we heard in the account from the gospel of Matthew (1:18-25). **Godly waiting is rarely easy but Godly waiting is always renewing and strengthening.**

Although waiting on God is rarely easy, it is supremely worthwhile. Godly waiting is always purposeful, always formative, always preparatory. Waiting on God or, better yet, waiting *in* God, enables trust to be built and strength to be increased. We learn how to rely on God rather than doing things ourselves. We learn to live and work in God's power rather than in our own power. **Let us ring our bells as a way of calling each other to this type of holy waiting in the context of a season which tempts us to give up waiting and entices us with myriad activities that ultimately will not strengthen but only frustrate and drain us.** *(Pastor and people ring their bells.)*

May God help us to wait with anticipation as we seek to be honest about our lives and our need for God's intervention on our behalf. May the Lord give us courage to wait with hope and confidence, knowing that God is our Advocate, not our adversary; God is for us, not against us; God's name is Emmanuel, which means "God is with us" (Matthew 1:23).

Let us pray. Great and Gracious God, thank you for being with us. We praise you for the promise that you will never leave nor forsake us. You have chosen us. We are yours, forever. Guide us through this Advent season of waiting, that we may be formed and transformed by the birth of Jesus Christ. Prepare us to receive him into our hearts and lives afresh. We pray these things in the name of Jesus who is our Savior, Lord, and Emmanuel. Amen.

---

1. Harris, R. Laird, Gleason L. Archer, Jr., and Bruce K. Waltke. *Theological Wordbook of the Old Testament*. Chicago: Moody Press, 1980, p. 791.

Second Sunday In Advent

Introduction to this Service:

Everyone is asked to bring **a candle** and **a candle holder** with them to worship. Additional candles should be provided for those who forget or did not know. The kind of candle used at many Christmas Eve services with the paper drip guard works well. The theme of the service is that Jesus Christ is the light of the world and so are we. Jesus served as a luminary, a light, a beacon for people to find their way to a saving belief in God. Jesus was the light of the world. But Jesus also called his followers to be the light of the world (Matthew 5:14-16).

Listeners are invited to think about a person or persons who have served as reflections of the light of Christ in their lives. These luminous individuals, while making no claim to being perfect, have represented what is good, noble, righteous, caring, and godly. People are encouraged to give thanks to God for those who have been Christ's light to them and to let them know how much their lives and Christian witness have meant.

The challenge is made to begin to be Christ's light in the world as we are and where we are. The Lord Jesus Christ wants each of us to be a light, now. If we will offer Christ ourselves, he will take our offering and transform us into light which brings glory to God.

CELEBRATING THE LORD'S DAY
SECOND SUNDAY IN ADVENT

OPENING SENTENCE 1 John 1:5-7

"This is the message we have heard from him and proclaim to you, that God is light and in him there is no darkness at all. If we say that we have fellowship with him while we are walking in darkness, we lie and do not do what is true; but if we walk in the light as he himself is in the light, we have fellowship with one another, and the blood of Jesus his Son cleanses us from all sin."

PRELUDE "Starlight"
Keith Thomas

PARISH ANNOUNCEMENTS

*WELCOMING ONE ANOTHER

Shake hands with those around you. Introduce yourself to those you do not know by name. Please remain standing for the "Gathering."

*GATHERING "Adoration"
Randy Vader

*ADVENT WREATH CANDLE LIGHTING CEREMONY

Leader: The people who walked in darkness have seen a great light; those who lived in a land of deep darkness — on them has light shined. (Isaiah 9:2)

People: Lord, send us your light that we might see. Send us your Son that we might be free.

Leader: We light the Advent Candles in expectation that Jesus Christ, the light of the world, is coming again. *(Light two candles.)*

People: Praise be to you, Lord Jesus Christ, who was, who is, and who is to come! Amen.

HYMN "Shine, Jesus, Shine"
Graham Kendrick

CHILDREN'S MESSAGE

GIVING OF TITHES AND OFFERING

OFFERTORY ANTHEM "The Birthday of a King"
W.H. Neidlinger

PRAYER OF CONFESSION

Gracious and forgiving God, in this Advent Season we are called upon to set aside time to worship you and make new commitments. We need to take time to turn from our sin, reflect on your gifts to us, and consider how we might best dedicate ourselves to you once again. Forgive us for being consumed with other agenda that pushes you to the margins of our lives. As we consider the privilege and joy of lighting candles in recognition that you are the light of the world, so also help us to honor your expectation that we be your lights in the world for others. Make this season truly holy for us. We pray these things in the name of Jesus Christ. Amen.

PRAYER SONGS

"Arise, Shine" Steven Urspringer and Jay Robinson
"Emmanuel, Emmanuel" Bob McGee

MORNING PRAYER and LORD'S PRAYER

ANTHEM "Arise, Shine, for Your Light Has Come"
Vader

*FIRST GOSPEL LESSON — John 8:12, 9:1-11

Leader: This is the Word of the Lord.
People: Thanks be to God. Amen.

*SECOND GOSPEL LESSON — Matthew 5:14-16

Leader: This is the Gospel of our Lord.
People: Praise be to you, Lord Jesus Christ. Amen.

*HYMN — "Hark! The Herald Angels Sing"
Charles Wesley

MORNING MESSAGE — "Let Your Light Shine"

CANDLE LIGHTING

Please keep the lighted candles upright and tip the unlighted candles as you pass the light along your row. Watch that no clothing or hair gets near the flame. At the conclusion of our hymn and blessing we will sing "Shalom" and raise our candles. Please extinguish them after "Shalom" but take the light of Christ with you into the world.

*HYMN — "I Want to Walk as a Child of the Light"
Kathleen Thomerson

*BLESSING

Go forth to reflect Christ's light in a darkened world that is searching for light, truth, and meaning. Know that the Lord loves you and desires to use you daily in being light for others. Amen.

*SHALOM — Roger N. Deschner

*BLESSING ONE ANOTHER and POSTLUDE

"O Magnify the Lord" — Dick and Melodie Tunney

*All who are able please stand

John 8:12, 9:1-11; Matthew 5:14-16

Let Your Light Shine

On this, the second Sunday of Advent, our worship is centered around the theme of light. The Gospel of John is filled with references to light. In the prologue of the Gospel, John 1:1-5, we encounter these words:

> *In the beginning was the Word, and the Word was with God, and the Word was God. He was in the beginning with God. All things came into being through him, and without him not one thing came into being. What has come into being in him was life, and the life was the* ***light*** *of all people. The* ***light*** *shines in the darkness, and the darkness did not overcome it.*
>
> (emphasis added)

A few verses later in John 1:9 we read, "The true light, which enlightens everyone, was coming into the world." To whom is the author referring? John is referring to Jesus Christ. The morning lesson from John 8:12 makes this explicit. Jesus said, "I am the light of the world. Whoever follows me will never walk in darkness but will have the light of life." Again, in John 9:5 Jesus stated, "As long as I am in the world, I am the light of the world."

Jesus' role of bringing light to a world in darkness is portrayed throughout the Gospel of John. One vivid story which is found in John chapter nine is of Jesus healing the man born blind. This man had walked in literal darkness for his entire life. The man's condition of blindness was used to make clear that Jesus was the light and that his light was not just figurative but literal. Jesus had power to bring light to those in physical darkness as well as those in spiritual and emotional darkness.

At first, everyone was in awe. They could hardly believe that the man before them was the one born blind. No one had ever been healed of a condition such as this (see John 9:32). The fellow was then brought to the religious authorities who could certify his healing. A great controversy arose because the man had been healed on the Sabbath; work of any kind, including good work, was considered to be unlawful on the Sabbath. What began as something worthy of praise and thanksgiving became ugly and controversial.

Those who saw themselves as defenders and preservers of the faith became resisters of God and deniers of Jesus the Messiah, God's Son. So certain were they of their own ability to discern truth from falsehood, good from evil, they stopped trusting in God and, instead, trusted in their own understanding and righteousness. They refused to accept the new understandings of the faith that God was trying to show them in the life and ministry of Jesus. Claiming to be children of the light they, in fact, dwelled in darkness, while those who recognized they were living in sin and darkness openly and gladly received Jesus, God's Light for the world (see John 9:39-41).

Jesus challenged the religious *status quo* of his day. He shook things up. He made people rethink their faith and the way they were living. He served as a luminary, a light, a beacon for people to find their way to a saving belief in God. Jesus was the light of the world.

Jesus said, "As long as I am in the world, I am the light of the world" (John 9:5). We realize that Jesus was crucified in the first century. Because of this, some might say that the light is no longer here. Would you agree?

Thoughtful Christians would probably reply, "No and yes." Why is this? While it is true that Jesus died nineteen centuries ago, it is also true that he rose from the dead on the third day following his crucifixion on the cross. Although it is true that Jesus is no longer with us in the flesh, we affirm that he is alive and at work in us and our world through the Holy Spirit, which he sent to be with us following his ascension into heaven. While Jesus, the person, is no longer with us, the Spirit of Jesus is very much alive and working through the agency of the church, Christian organizations, and people of faith.

This leads us to affirm that not only is Jesus the light of the world, but so are *we*. Jesus claimed precisely this in Matthew 5:14-16:

> ***You*** *are the light of the world. A city built on a hill cannot be hid. No one after lighting a lamp puts it under the bushel basket, but on the lampstand, and it gives light to all in the house. In the same way, let your light shine before others, so that they may see your good works and give glory to your Father in heaven.*
>
> (emphasis added)

If we think about it, most of us can identify a person or persons who have served as reflections of the light of God in our lives. These individuals, although making no claim to being perfect, have represented to us that which is good, noble, righteous, caring, and godly. On your bulletin write the names of these persons. I encourage you to give thanks to God for those who have been Christ's light for you. If they are alive, I hope you will call, visit, or write to them in the coming week to let them know how much they have meant to you. Tell them how they have been God's light and love to you.

I now want to share a secret with you. It is a simple secret. Let Christ use *you* to be a light *where you are*. Don't wait to start being a light until you get your life all sorted out or all your problems fixed. If you wait, you will never get started! You will miss the simple, yet profound opportunity to influence and shape the lives of those closest to you. The Lord Jesus Christ wants you to be a light, now. If you will offer him yourself, he will take your offering and transform you into light which brings glory to God. He will help you step outside old patterns that hinder and bind just as he did the blind man and the religious leaders of his day. I encourage you to resolve today to be Christ's light in the world. You can make a difference! Take a moment now to write in your bulletin what you can do to light a candle to be a light to someone.

(You can end the message here or close by using an illustration of someone who has been a light for you and made a difference in your life. An alternative would be to obtain the story titled "A Candle in the Darkness."[1])

This story is about a nineteen-year-old boy by the name of Daniel Gavra whose Christian faith led him to light a candle in the darkness to protest the oppressive regime of the notorious dictator, Ceausescu, in Romania. His courage and that of others in the face of great personal suffering galvanized a nation to rise up and overthrow the communist government. Daniel helped to spark a revolution that is still being felt today. Romania is a democratic country thanks to the effort of people like Daniel Gavra who were willing to put their lives on the line for the sake of the Gospel and for basic human rights.

You and I can make a difference where we are if we are willing to take a stand. Don't wait for someone else to do it. Be the first to light *your candle*. And let your light shine!

Let us pray. Dear God, we have been blessed, touched, inspired and warmed by the light others have shared with us. Help us now to take our light, to lift it up with courage and conviction. May we embrace the wonderful secret of the light of Christ: that you can and will use us as we are and where we are. Help us to begin now, not when we think we are ready. Awaken us to the simple yet profound opportunities to influence and shape the lives of those closest to us. Grant us courage to offer ourselves, our talents and resources, so that you can take our gifts and transform them into light which will bring glory to you, O God. Just as Jesus did for the blind man and religious leaders of his day, help us to be free from old, no longer faithful patterns that hinder and bind. Lord, we want to be Christ's light in the world. Help us to make a difference. In Jesus' name we pray. Amen.

---

1. Rice, Wayne. *More Hot Illustrations for Youth Talks.* Grand Rapids, MI: Youth Specialties, Zondervan Publishing House, 1995, pp. 17-18.

Third Sunday In Advent

Introduction to this Service:

People should be told to come to church **prepared to offer a gift** either of money or a present that has been purchased for a mission of your choosing. The theme of worship on this third Sunday of Advent is gifts. Jesus is God's gift to the world. We, in turn, are to be God's gift to others.

When we give gifts at this time of year, it is a way of remembering what God has done for us and for all humanity, and an opportunity to celebrate the gift of God's Son, Jesus. To give gifts, therefore, is to live in the Spirit of God. An emphasis is placed on the importance of expressing gratitude for the gifts we receive.

You will need to have a wrapped gift of your own for use as a visual illustration in the message. A bulletin insert which is to be used as a sermon listening guide can be found after the sermon text. At the conclusion of the message, people are invited to come forward with their gifts and place them on the altar.

THIRD SUNDAY IN ADVENT
CELEBRATING THE LORD'S DAY

OPENING SENTENCE Matthew 1:20-21, 24

"An angel of the Lord appeared in a dream, saying, 'Joseph, son of David, do not fear to take Mary your wife, for that which is conceived in her is of the Holy Spirit; she will bear a son, and you shall call his name Jesus, for he will save his people from their sins.' When Joseph woke from sleep, he did as the angel of the Lord commanded him."

PRELUDE "Gesu Bambino"
arr. Juliet Calkins

PARISH ANNOUNCEMENTS

*WELCOMING ONE ANOTHER
Shake hands with those around you. Introduce yourself to those you do not know by name. Please remain standing for the "Gathering."

*GATHERING "Adoration"
Randy Vader

*ADVENT WREATH CANDLE LIGHTING CEREMONY

Leader: Jesus Christ is God's gift to the world. We, in turn, are to be God's gift to others.

People: When we give gifts at this time of year, it is a way of remembering what God has done for us and for all humanity, and an opportunity to celebrate the gift of God's Son, Jesus. To give gifts, therefore, is to live in the Spirit of God.

Leader: This morning we light the three Advent Candles in celebration of the gift of God's Son, Jesus.

People: We come to worship and adore him who is Christ the Lord. Amen. *(Leader lights three candles.)*

HYMN "O Come, All Ye Faithful"
John F. Wade

CHILDREN'S MESSAGE

GIVING OF TITHES AND OFFERING

OFFERTORY ANTHEM "The First Noel/
It Came Upon The Midnight Clear"
arr. Tedd Smith

PRAYER OF CONFESSION

Gracious and forgiving God, in this Advent Season we are called upon to set aside time to worship you and make new commitments. We need to take time to turn from our sin, reflect on your gifts to us, and consider how we might best dedicate ourselves to you once again. Forgive us for being consumed with other agenda that pushes you to the margins of our lives. As we consider the privilege and joy of bringing gifts for others in joyful response to the gift of your Son, Jesus Christ, help us to offer ourselves freely and without reservation. Make this season truly holy for us. We pray these things in the name of Jesus Christ. Amen.

PRAYER SONG "More Precious Than Silver"
Lynn DeShazo

MORNING PRAYER and LORD'S PRAYER

ANTHEM

*FIRST GOSPEL LESSON Luke 1:26-38, 2:8-20

Leader: This is the Word of the Lord.
People: Thanks be to God. Amen.

*SECOND GOSPEL LESSON Matthew 2:1-12

Leader: This is the Gospel of our Lord.
People: Praise be to you, Lord Jesus Christ. Amen.

*HYMN "O Little Town of Bethlehem"
Phillips Brooks

MORNING MESSAGE "G.I.F.T."

*HYMN "The First Noel"
Trad. English Carol

During the singing of the hymn, please come down the center aisle with your gift and place it in front of the altar. You may return to your seat by the side aisle.

*BLESSING

Let us go forth to share with others in the same manner we have received — freely, generously, with a heart full of gratitude and praise for the blessings of God that have been richly bestowed upon us in Christ Jesus. Amen.

*BLESSING ONE ANOTHER and POSTLUDE

*All who are able please stand

Luke 1:26-38, 2:8-20; Matthew 2:1-12

G.I.F.T.

The seasons of Advent and Christmas are times when gifts are on our minds. We purchase or make gifts as an expression of love and appreciation. We write letters and send cards. We wrap presents and pray special blessings on those who have meant a lot to us. We receive gifts of all kinds from family and friends. We celebrate with festive meals, distinctive foods, and gala outings such as concerts, plays, and cantatas. We sing favorite carols, light special candles, decorate trees, hang wreaths, bows, and ornaments, and enjoy a host of traditions.

(Recount one of your favorite holiday traditions.)

The tradition of giving gifts at this time of year arose from the New Testament. We give gifts because doing so is in keeping with what God did for us when he sent his Son Jesus, the Christ, to the world. John 3:16 says, "For God so loved the world that he ***gave*** his only Son, so that everyone who believes in him may not perish but may have eternal life" (emphasis added). **Our God is a gift-giving God.** When we give gifts at this time of year, it is a way of remembering what God has done for us and for all humanity, and an opportunity to celebrate the gift of God's Son, Jesus. To give gifts, therefore, is to live in the Spirit of God. What a blessing and joy it is for us to live in the Spirit of God!

Admittedly, there are and always have been dangers to giving gifts. We can get so caught up with a sense of obligation to give that we forget the privilege of giving. We can become so enamored with gifts that we forget to pause and give thanks for the love and regard being expressed beyond the gifts themselves. We can lose sight of the fact that God's gift of Jesus was what prompted the tradition of giving gifts in the first place. Despite the dangers, however, the act of giving and receiving gifts is important for us all.

The story of the wise men seeing a new star in the sky and coming from the East to worship Jesus is a story about the value of receiving and giving gifts. The story is about *receiving* gifts because the wise men first had to see the star, recognize its importance, and journey hundreds of miles across the desert and wilderness to Bethlehem. The story is also about *giving* gifts. The wise men brought gifts that were appropriate to give honor and pay tribute to Christ, the newborn king. They brought the gifts of gold, frankincense, and myrrh.

Each of these gifts was symbolic of who Jesus was. **The gold symbolized Jesus' royalty.** He was born the king of the Jews and the hope of the world. **The frankincense was symbolic of Jesus' deity.** He was not merely a human being; he was and is the Son of God. **The myrrh was symbolic of Jesus' destiny.** He was given by God to the world to die on the cross so that all who believe in him might not suffer the penalty of their sin but, through faith in him, receive forgiveness for their sin and inherit the promise of eternal life.

In keeping with the spirit of giving which characterized Jesus' beginnings, his life, and his final hours, I want to suggest three acronyms. In an acronym, each letter stands for a different word. You will find these acronyms on the bulletin insert. Please turn there at this time.

The first acronym is G.I.F.T. After the *G* write God. After the *I* write Incarnate. After the *F* write Forever. After the *T* write Thankful. **G.I.F.T. means "God incarnate forever thankful."** The gift which we celebrate in this season is the gift of God becoming a human being. "Incarnate" means "embodied in flesh." Jesus Christ is God incarnate; God embodied in flesh. The appropriate and faithful response to the gift of God being embodied in the flesh, in the person of Jesus Christ, is eternal gratitude.

Think about how you have felt, having cared enough to give a gift, when the recipient was not particularly thankful. It does not feel very good. In truth, it hurts. Showing gratitude and recognizing the effort on the part of the giver are important to acknowledge.

Teaching children the importance of writing Christmas "thank you" cards within a few days of opening their gifts is invaluable.

While they may not fully understand or appreciate the significance of expressing gratitude unconditionally, it will bless the giver and may help the child as he or she grows older — with common courtesy as well as having a thankful attitude.

When children are excited about their gifts, the notes may read something like what a little boy wrote:

> *Dear Grandma and Grandpa,*
>
> *Thank you for the rifle, six shooter, lariat, and cowboy hat. They are the best! I have had great fun tying up my brother and sisters. They are also learning how to fall down when I shoot. The only trouble is they don't stay down! I hope you had a very Merry Christmas.*
>
> *Love, Johnny*

Contrast this to the note when the child is not very excited about the gift. The attempt is still made to at least *sound grateful.* It might read something like the note from the child who wrote:

> *Dear Aunt Esther,*
>
> *Thank you for the big bag of hard candy, the new underwear, and bright red Christmas socks. I also appreciate the two dollars you sent me. I will use it for something special.*
>
> *Love, Jim*

What Jim wanted to tell Aunt Esther was that he never has liked hard candy, that underwear as a gift is embarrassing for a kid, and that he will never put on the red socks again (after his parents *made him* wear them on Christmas morning while he was acting as Santa). In all likelihood, Jim probably does want to tell his aunt, "Why don't you make it easy on yourself next year and just send money?"

Writing awkward thank you notes, as difficult and contrived as they sometimes are, helps us to get in touch with the realization that the giver tried to bless us. Often, the giver wants to get us something useful, something that would make us happy. The trouble is that they may not know us very well. Despite this, the person has given a gift. A thank you note is a significant way for children as well as adults to graciously acknowledge the gift and the one who gave it.

Friends, God has given you and me a gift, a lovely gift filled with meaning and significance, a gift which was sent with each of us in mind. Perhaps you have not felt much need for this gift, preferring that God would have sent something more useful, something more to your liking. Maybe you have responded to God like Jim did with some of Aunt Esther's gifts, half-heartedly, unenthusiastically. Perhaps you have ignored the gift of God altogether. Despite the gift having your name on it, maybe you thought it was for someone else. Maybe you did not think you were worthy of the gift. Could it be that something within you has caused you to ignore or overlook the gift of God? Isn't it time to take another look at the gift of God this Christmas? Isn't it time to express some thanks to God for at least trying to bless you? Maybe, just maybe, if you will take the time to open and receive the gift of God, you will discover it is more to your liking than you originally thought! Taking time to acknowledge God's gift and offer a word of thanks will bless God. To your surprise, it might even bless you.

When we give a gift *(take out wrapped gift)*, the recipient sees our face. When we write a "thank you" note, the receiver pictures our face in their minds. In like manner, the gift of God is *not* an impersonal gift. God's gift has a face, a human face, the face of Jesus. In Jesus Christ, God became like you and me in every way. Jesus knew how to laugh, he knew how to have a good time, and he knew how to cry. He was acknowledged and accepted by some, criticized and rejected by others. He lived and loved to the fullest. He became like us in every way except one. He was without sin. God became like us, so that we could become God's children.

We read in 1 John 3:1-3:

> *See what love the Father has given us, that we should be called children of God; and so we are. The reason why*

the world does not know us is that it did not know him. Beloved, we are God's children now; it does not yet appear what we shall be, but we know that when he appears we shall be like him, for we shall see him as he is. And every one who thus hopes in him purifies himself as he is pure.

Turning back to the bulletin insert, the acronym for **F.A.C.E. stands for Foretold, Accepted, Celebrated, and Encountered.** I will illustrate each one of these so that you can write down the word and a biblical reference. *F* stands for Foretold. Jesus' birth was foretold by the Old Testament prophet Isaiah. Isaiah 7:14 says, "Behold, a virgin shall conceive and bear a son, and shall call his name Immanuel." In Isaiah 9:6 we find the now familiar words, "For to us a child is born, to us a son is given; and the government will be upon his shoulder, and his name will be called 'Wonderful Counselor, Mighty God, Everlasting Father, Prince of Peace.' "

This gift of God was also foretold to Mary, the mother of Jesus, by the angel Gabriel. "Do not be afraid, Mary, for you have found favor with God. And behold, you will conceive in your womb and bear a son, and you shall call his name Jesus" (Luke 1:30-31).

The gift was not only foretold but also accepted. The *A* in F.A.C.E. stands for Accepted. Jesus' birth, despite its unusual origins, was accepted by Mary and Joseph. Mary said, "Behold, I am the handmaid of the Lord; let it be to me according to your word" (Luke 1:37). Joseph had a more difficult time with his wife-to-be being pregnant, but he too accepted the birth of Jesus. In a dream an angel told him not to be afraid of taking Mary to be his wife ...

"for that which is conceived in her is of the Holy Spirit; she will bear a son, and you shall call his name Jesus, for he will save his people from their sins." ... When Joseph woke from sleep, he did as the angel of the Lord commanded him....

(Matthew 1:20-24)

The *C* in F.A.C.E. stands for Celebrated. In the Gospel of Luke, from which we read this morning, it is told how an angel visited shepherds in the fields outside of Bethlehem the night that Jesus was born. After the wonderful, awe-inspiring announcement of Christ's birth, a great host of angels appeared, singing, "Glory to God in the highest heaven, and on earth peace among those whom he favors" (Luke 2:14). Acceptance and celebration are very appropriate responses to the gift of God which was foretold in the Scriptures and heralded by angels.

The *E* in F.A.C.E. stands for Encountered. Having heard the celebration of Jesus' birth by the angels, the shepherds went with haste to Bethlehem to see the things that the Lord had made known to them. When they arrived, they found Mary and Joseph and the child lying in the manger. They reported the glorious things which the angels had told them. Then, returning to their fields and their flocks, they glorified God for all they had seen and heard (Luke 2:16-20).

I have already mentioned the wise men. They too came and encountered the baby Jesus who was the Son of God. They gave him gifts and homage worthy of One whose royalty, deity, and destiny came from God (Matthew 2:1-12).

Each of us needs a personal encounter with Jesus Christ the King. He is not dead but lives and reigns today. He is not far off, distant, or inaccessible. Rather, he is nearer than a breath and closer than a prayer. He is known as "Emmanuel," which means "God is with us." This gift of God has a human face. He became like us. Therefore, he understands your situation and mine. You can trust him with your life. What will be your response to the birth of Jesus Christ?

This leads us to the third acronym, R.E.S.P.O.N.S.E. I will tell you briefly what each letter stands for and then we will conclude with prayer. The *R* is for Rejoice. We respond best to God's "gift with a human face" by rejoicing. The *E* is for Emmanuel. This gift of God is unlike any other. In Jesus, God has promised to be "with us" always. The *S* stands for Son and Savior. Jesus was more than a good person. He was and is God's Son and our Savior. The *P* stands for Purchased. The *O* is for Our. God's gifts are always personally addressed and given to you and me. The *N* is for Never failing. The *S* is for Salvation. We are saved from the eternal consequences of sin by believing in and receiving Jesus Christ for our salvation. The *E* stands for Eternally. As a whole, the acronym **R.E.S.P.O.N.S.E. stands for "Rejoice, Emmanuel, Son and Savior, Purchased Our Never Failing Salvation Eternally."**

Friends, I invite you to accept the gift of God this Christmas. God's gift has a human face and calls us for a response of deep thanksgiving and heartfelt gratitude. Receiving this gift, God's gift of his Son Jesus, will change your life for the best, forever.

Let us pray. We rejoice, O God, in your countless gifts to us, and most especially for the gift of your Son Jesus. With gratitude and thanksgiving, we invite Christ into our lives, whether it be for the first time or the hundredth time. Father, just as all kinds of people encountered you and worshiped you that first Christmas, so now lead us into a divine encounter once again. Help us to live and love in such ways as to lead others to him.

Bless the gifts that we now bring for those less fortunate. May these gifts be tangible symbols of our caring and your generous love. We ask this through your Son, our Savior and Lord, Jesus Christ. Amen.

Sermon Listening Guide

G -

I -

F -

T -

F -

A -

C -

E -

R -

E -

S -

P -

O -

N -

S -

E -

Fourth Sunday In Advent

Introduction to this Service:

On this fourth Sunday of Advent, joy is theme of the service. Everyone is asked to bring **a joyful spirit** and **a willingness to sing to the Lord.** Not everyone feels what we commonly associate with joy. The holidays are difficult for some people. A meaning of joy that does not rely on pleasant circumstances is explored in this message.

People may wonder what joy is, true joy, godly joy. We get a sense of the meaning of joy by hearing some contrasts. True joy is oftentimes quiet rather than loud; subtle rather than brazen; deep versus superficial; God-centered instead of self-centered; God-made rather than self-made; spiritually based versus circumstantially based.

The message explores each of the verses of Mary's song, called the Magnificat, found in Luke 1:47-56. A contrasting viewpoint is then offered which reflects the perspective of many people in the world.

For people of faith, true joy is found in doing things God's way and trusting that God's way is right for all persons. We realize that emptiness is found in every other way, so we commit and recommit ourselves to God's way, despite what it costs us. In so doing, Mary's song of joy can become *our* song. The key to making it so is being able to rejoice in God's presence and providence regardless of our circumstances. It is learning to affirm the spiritual significance and fruitful possibilities to be found in our difficulties and suffering, instead of waiting for fair weather and pleasant circumstances. To do so will assure that the gift of true joy, born of faith, will become our song.

FOURTH SUNDAY IN ADVENT
CELEBRATING THE LORD'S DAY

OPENING SENTENCE Luke 1:47-48

Mary, the mother of Jesus, said, "My soul magnifies the Lord, and my spirit rejoices in God my Savior, for he has looked with favor on the lowliness of his servant...."

PRELUDE "Joy to the World" with "Psalm 19"
arr. Linda McKechnie

PARISH ANNOUNCEMENTS

*WELCOMING ONE ANOTHER

Shake hands with those around you. Introduce yourself to those you do not know by name. Please remain standing for the "Gathering."

*GATHERING "Adoration"
Randy Vader

*ADVENT WREATH CANDLE LIGHTING CEREMONY

(Based on Psalm 96:1-4)

Leader: O sing to the Lord a new song;

People: Sing to the Lord, all the earth.

Leader: Sing to the Lord, bless God's name;

People: Tell of God's salvation from day to day.

Leader: Declare God's glory among the nations,

People: God's marvelous works among all the people.

Leader: For great is the Lord, and greatly to be praised;

People: God is to be revered above all gods.

Leader: We light the fourth Advent candle as a symbol of joy.

People: Thanks be to God! *(Leader lights four candles.)*

HYMNS

"Angels We Have Heard on High" (vv. 1 and 2)
Trad. French Carol

"There's a Song in the Air" (vv. 1, 2, and 4)
Josiah G. Holland

"Angels from the Realms of Glory" (vv. 1 and 2)
James Montgomery

CHILDREN'S MESSAGE

GIVING OF TITHES AND OFFERING

OFFERTORY ANTHEM "The Manger Medley"
arr. Fred Bock

PRAYER OF CONFESSION

Gracious and forgiving God, in this Advent Season we are called upon to set aside time to worship you and make new commitments. We need to take time to turn from our sin, reflect on your gifts to us, and consider how we might best dedicate ourselves to you once again. Forgive us for being consumed with other agenda that pushes you to the margins of our lives. Today, it is our privilege to rejoice in your holy name. Cleanse the thoughts and intentions of our hearts, that we may sing your praises. Make this season truly holy for us. We ask this through Christ our Lord. Amen.

PRAYER SONG "Come, Thou Long Expected Jesus"
Charles Wesley

MORNING PRAYER and LORD'S PRAYER

ANTHEM "Born in Bethlehem"
arr. Kirkland

*FIRST GOSPEL LESSON Luke 1:39-56

Leader: This is the Word of the Lord.
People: Thanks be to God. Amen.

*SECOND GOSPEL LESSON Luke 2:25-32

Leader: This is the Gospel of our Lord.
People: Praise be to you, Lord Jesus Christ. Amen.

*HYMNS

"The Child of Bethlehem" Dan Burgess
"Morning Star" Dan Burgess

MORNING MESSAGE "Sing To The Lord"

*HYMN "Joy to the World"
Isaac Watts

*BLESSING

Go forth to share your joy with the world. May the Spirit of Jesus so live in you that people may see your good and faithful works and give glory to God. Amen.

*BLESSING ONE ANOTHER and POSTLUDE

*All who are able please stand

Luke 1:39-56

Sing To The Lord

Psalm 96 begins with these words:

> *O sing to the Lord a new song; sing to the Lord, all the earth. Sing to the Lord, bless his name; tell of his salvation from day to day. Declare his glory among the nations, his marvelous works among all the peoples. For great is the Lord, and greatly to be praised; he is to be revered above all gods.*
>
> (vv. 1-4)

In listening to this Psalm there is a sense of joy, a feeling of glad celebration. On the fourth Sunday of Advent, this is the spirit that should characterize our worship. We are to have a spirit of joy.

What is joy, true joy, godly joy? We can get a sense of the meaning of joy by hearing some contrasts. True joy is oftentimes quiet rather than loud; subtle rather than brazen; deep versus superficial; God-centered instead of self-centered; God-made rather than self-made; spiritually based versus circumstantially based.

Mary's song, which we read this morning in the Gospel of Luke, is a song of true joy. This song is called the "Magnificat" because of the opening line: "My soul magnifies the Lord, and my spirit rejoices in God my Savior" (Luke 1:47). What a contrast this is to what Mary could have been feeling! She could have justifiably said, "I feel alone and depressed. I left my hometown to escape ridicule and ostracism because of my pregnancy." Instead, Mary's song is filled with hope, confidence in God, and trust in God's plan and God's provision.

This morning we will explore together each of the verses of Mary's song to get a fuller sense of her joy, which is in sharp contrast to her circumstances. I invite you to open your Bible to Luke 1:47-56. I will read a verse at a time of the Magnificat and then offer a contrasting viewpoint which reflects the perspective of many in the world.

We have already examined and contrasted verse 47. The first part of verse 48 reads, "For He has looked with favor on the lowliness of his servant." Mary could have said, "I am now homeless and living just a step away from poverty and starvation." Instead, she is mindful of the honor God has bestowed on her when the angel Gabriel came and said, "Greetings, favored one! The Lord is with you ... Do not be afraid, Mary, for you have found favor with God" (Luke 1:28, 30).

The second part of verse 48 and verse 49 read, "Surely, from now on all generations will call me blessed; for the Mighty One has done great things for me, and holy is his name." Mary could have bemoaned the fact that she was pregnant out of wedlock and her husband-to-be was not very happy about it. Instead, her focus is on God and God's great blessing upon her life which is explained in Luke 1:35: "The Holy Spirit will come upon you, and the power of the Most High will overshadow you; therefore the child to be born will be holy; he will be called Son of God."

Verse 50 reads, "His mercy is for those who fear him from generation to generation." The wisdom of the world suggests something quite different. Conventional wisdom says, "Life is up to us and what we make of it." There is no comprehension that "the fear of the Lord is the beginning of wisdom and knowledge of the Holy One is insight" (Proverbs 9:10). This fear does not mean that we should be terrified of God as a child is of an abusive parent. Rather, the Greek word for "fear" means that we should have a holy awe, a reverence for the Lord. God's mercy is upon those who reverence him from generation to generation.

In verse 51 Mary says, "He has shown strength with his arm; he has scattered the proud in the thoughts of their hearts." In contrast, conventional wisdom suggests, "You only go around once in life. You have to grab for all the gusto you can." "The one who has the most toys at the end wins." We know that pride comes before the fall. Why is it that we insist on being stubbornly prideful, and self-sufficient, even when we know that it is counter-productive? Mary's relationship with God is starkly different. It was characterized by holy humility and absolute trust in God's power and provision.

The powerful in the world offer a completely different message: "You need to take charge to be successful. Exercise control. Don't let anyone else get the upper hand." Mary, in verse 52, says, "He has brought down the powerful from their thrones, and lifted up the lowly." How would people characterize you? Are you the type of person who is most comfortable exercising power? Or are you willing to be a servant leader? Where is it that you need to give some consideration for change in your style of living in order that a greater measure of authentic joy might be yours?

We find in verse 53, "He has filled the hungry with good things, and sent the rich away empty." Many of us have the attitude that we need to take care of ourselves because no one else will. This attitude runs completely counter to the message of Scripture. If this hits home, perhaps we need to learn to trust God. Giving a tithe to God, ten percent or more of our earnings, is a tangible sign of our readiness to recognize God's ownership of all we have and our willingness to rely on God for all our needs.

Mary concludes her song with a declaration of faith, "He has helped his servant Israel, in remembrance of his mercy, according to the promise he made to our ancestors, to Abraham and to his descendants forever" (vv. 54-55). Mary's song, together with the story of the Scripture as a whole, is a testimony of God helping those who are God's servants. The biblical story is one of God remembering the promises made to our foreparents and continuing to honor these promises with those who live in this lineage. In radical contrast, conventional wisdom would want us to believe that we cannot trust anyone, that God only helps those who help themselves, and that we must distinguish ourselves or we will be forgotten and our life will not amount to anything.

For people of faith, true joy is found in doing things God's way and trusting that God's way is right for all of us. We realize that emptiness is found in every other way, so we commit and recommit ourselves to God's way, despite what it costs us. In so doing, Mary's song of joy can become *our* song. The key to making it so is being able to rejoice in God's presence and providence regardless of our circumstances. We need to be able to affirm the spiritual significance and fruitful possibilities to be found in our difficulties and suffering, instead of waiting for fair weather and pleasant circumstances. To do so will assure that true joy, born of faith, will become our song.

Let me illustrate this with a story. It was in the midst of adversity, 178 years ago, that two men found a song to sing to the Lord. The young pastor was sad. As he strolled across the snow-covered slopes above his village of Oberndorf, Austria, he reflected on the predicament. In a few days it would be Christmas Eve, but Pastor Joseph Mohr knew there would be no music in his church to herald the great event. The new organ, recently installed in the church, had broken down. Mice had chewed through the leather bellows, rendering it useless.

Pastor Mohr paused in his evening walk. He looked down at the scattered lights of the village below. The sight of the peaceful town, huddled warmly in the foothills, stirred his imagination. Surely it was on such a clear and quiet night as this that hosts of angels sang out the glorious news that the Savior had been born. The young pastor sighed, "If only we here in Oberndorf could celebrate the birth of Jesus with glorious music like the shepherds heard on that wonderful night!" As he reflected on this, his mind filled with visions of that first Christmas. The disappointment about the organ gave way to new inspiration! In his mind he could see Mary and Joseph kneeling in front of the manger; there was the Christ Child. The thoughts began to form themselves into a poem. He went home and wrote it down. The next day he went to the home of Franz Gruber, the church organist. The excited organist said, "These words could be sung at Christmas!" "But with the organ broken," said Pastor Mohr, "what instrument can we use?" The organist reached for his guitar and looked up at the pastor. Pastor Mohr then said, "Like Mary and Joseph in the stable, we must be content with what God provides for us." Franz Gruber studied the poem, then softly strummed the melody that came to him. Next he put the words to the melody and sang them. When he finished, his soul was ablaze with its beauty.

On Christmas Eve, 1818, in a small Austrian village, the Oberndorf choir, accompanied only by a guitar, sang for the first time the immortal and most beloved Christmas carol in the world, "Silent Night, Holy Night."

(If you have a person who plays guitar proficiently, invite him or her to accompany the church in the singing of the first two verses of "Silent Night, Holy Night." The mood of quiet joy and worship might best be kept if the congregation remains seated for the singing.)

Friends, God has given each of us a song to sing. The song is filled with a joy that is at times deep and quiet, as we have just experienced. At other times our joy is exuberant and glorious. Regardless of the type of joy, it is always centered in God and is a God-given gift rather than something made by humans. God's joy is spiritually based and has little to do with our circumstances being comfortable or easy. Let us ponder this in our hearts as we rise to sing together "Joy to the World." Amen.

Christmas Eve/Day

Introduction to this Service:

Many people struggle with having too much to do at Christmastime. The consequence is that we live harried lives in a season intended for us to welcome the Prince of Peace. People are invited to come to this worship bringing with them an attitude of openness and expectancy so as to experience God in new ways this Christmas.

This service is intended to assist persons to let go of their frantic busyness and intentionally relax in the presence of God. As they relax, a "thin" place is created, a place in which to experience God more deeply. They open themselves to the presence and power of God that is always available.

The approach of the message is to help people journey in their imaginations to several places in which God's presence has been experienced in profound ways. These places serve to remind us that God has been reaching out to humanity in many and varied ways across the ages.

The particular attitudes that are lifted up as most helpful in experiencing God afresh are humble awe, excited openness, willing obedience, and abundant rejoicing. Several stories are shared in the hope that people will see that God is not playing hide and seek with humanity. God is not playing a game of being hard to get with us. Instead, God has been at work in both ordinary and extraordinary events of life, creating "thin" places in which the divine and human are in close proximity, whereby humanity can encounter God in real, powerful, transformational ways. Our privilege and responsibility is to look for the ways that God is trying to reach us and our world and help others to respond to God as well.

CELEBRATING JESUS CHRIST'S BIRTH
CHRISTMAS EVE/DAY
A Service of Proclamation, Holy Communion, and Candlelight

CHRISTMAS PRELUDE MUSIC
(Allow 30 minutes for this prior to the service)

"Christmas Echoes"	Surdo
"The Shepherds and the Angels"	Lorenz
"The Birthday of a King"	Neidlinger
"He Shall Feed His Flock"	Handel
"Dearest, Lord Jesus"	J.S.Bach
"What Child Is This?"	English Carol-Greensleeves

ALTERNATIVE PRELUDE

"Angels We Have Heard on High" — arr. A.L. Page

GREETING — Luke 2:10-11

I bring you good news of great joy for all people: to you is born this day in the city of David a Savior, who is the Messiah, Christ, the Lord.

PROCESSION OF THE CAROLS
(We will sing the first verse of each carol from memory)

"O Come, All Ye Faithful"	John F. Wade
"O Little Town of Bethlehem"	Phillips Brooks
"Hark! The Herald Angels Sing"	Charles Wesley
"It Came Upon the Midnight Clear"	Edmund H. Sears
"The First Noel"	Trad. English Carol

THE LIGHTING OF THE CHRIST CANDLE
(Based upon Isaiah 9:2; Matthew 4:16)

Leader: "The people who walked in darkness have seen a great light; those who dwelt in a land of deep darkness, on them has light shined."

People: We gather with hearts full of reverence and praise. We come to worship the child who is God made flesh, the hope of the world.

Leader: We light the Christ candle to celebrate the birth of Jesus Christ, the light of the world.

People: Thanks be to God! Amen! *(Leader lights the Christ candle and the four Advent candles.)*

CHILDREN'S MESSAGE

PRAYER OF CONFESSION (Unison)

Gracious and forgiving God, on this day we gather to celebrate the gift of your Son, Jesus Christ. We confess our need to clear away the clutter of things that distract us from worshiping you. It is our desire to come before you in awe and adoration. Help us to worship you with a sense of expectancy and hope that you will meet us where we are and lead us to the place you want us to be. We offer our prayer in the name of Jesus Christ. Amen.

ANTHEM "Christmas Is a Time To Sing"

*FIRST GOSPEL LESSON Matthew 2:1-12

Leader: God always blesses the reading of the Word.

People: Lord, open our hearts to you.

*SECOND GOSPEL LESSON Luke 2:8-20

Leader: This is the Gospel of our Lord.

People: Praise be to you, Lord Jesus Christ. Amen.

SERMON "Changing The 'Too Much Syndrome' "

*HYMN "Joy to the World"
Isaac Watts

GIVING OF TITHES AND OFFERINGS

OFFERTORY ANTHEM "O Holy Night"
arr. W.E. Mercer

HOLY COMMUNION

LIGHTING OF THE CANDLES

For safety's sake never tip a lighted candle. Let the person with the unlit candle tip toward the lighted candle. Beware of hair or clothing near the flame. At the conclusion of the service, fully extinguish the candle with moistened fingertip or by blowing.

CAROL BY CANDLELIGHT "Silent Night"
Joseph Mohr

Silent Night, Holy Night, all is calm, all is bright
Round yon virgin mother and child;
Holy infant, so tender and mild,
Sleep in heavenly peace, sleep in heavenly peace.

Silent Night, Holy Night, shepherds quake at the sight;
Glories stream from heaven afar,
Heavenly hosts sing Alleluia;
Christ the Savior is born, Christ the Savior is born!

(Raise lighted candles during third stanza as a tribute to God's Wondrous Light shining in our lives.)

Silent Night, Holy Night, Son of God, love's pure light;
Radiant beams from thy holy face
With the dawn of redeeming grace,
Jesus, Lord, at thy birth; Jesus, Lord at thy birth.

Silent Night, Holy Night, wondrous Star, lend thy light;
With the angels let us sing,

Alleluia to our King.
Christ the Savior is born; Christ the Savior is born.

BLESSING | The Lord's Prayer

(In unison with eyes open)

Our Father, who art in heaven, hallowed be thy name. Thy kingdom come, thy will be done on earth as it is in heaven. Give us this day our daily bread. And forgive us our trespasses, as we forgive those who trespass against us. And lead us not into temptation, but deliver us from evil. For thine is the kingdom, and the power, and the glory, forever. Amen.

EXTINGUISHING OF THE CANDLES

POSTLUDE

Luke 2:8-20; Matthew 2:1-12

Changing The "Too Much Syndrome"

Everyone I know has something to say about the time leading up to Christmas. I have heard people say that this season involves too much busyness, too much fatigue, too much pressure, too much eating, drinking, baking, and buying. With all the hopes, expectations, traditions, obligations, dreams and fantasies that surround Christmas, it is easy to see why this time seems to be reduced to too much of almost everything.

I invite you to lay down and lay aside these experiences for the moment. This worship is an opportunity to let go of your harried rushing and relax in the presence of God and loved ones and, for a time, *receive* a gift instead of trying to give one. We hope this gift will help to transform the rest of your activities so that they will take on some of the qualities of the sacred and holy that are at the heart of Christmas.

Let's take a journey to some distant places and see what attitudes characterized some other people who celebrated Christmas. Then we can think about our own experience and perhaps find, with God's help, some meaningful alternatives to what I call the "too much syndrome."

First of all, let us journey in our minds to an isolated, rocky, windswept island off the West Coast of Scotland. Centuries ago Christians built a monastery on the island of Iona which became a vital mission station from which to evangelize the Scots. The testimony and faithfulness of the Christians at Iona Abbey impacted a nation, and its influence continues to be felt today.

The Scots call Iona a "thin" place. What they mean is that heaven and earth come close together in this place. In other words, God's presence is experienced there in a profound way. The result is that life is transformed, enriched, and made more peaceful, sacred, and holy by God's presence. Just the sound of a place like this seems inviting after six weeks of the "too much syndrome."

Let us take the idea of a "thin" place in our minds and journey down the coast of Europe to Rome, Italy. The image of another kind of "thin" place was depicted for us by the artist Michelangelo when he painted the vaulted ceiling of the Sistine Chapel. Perhaps some of you have seen it or seen pictures of this majestic work of art. In one scene, Michelangelo depicts God reaching with a strong, outstretched arm toward Adam, the first human. Adam is also reaching, but with bent elbow, somewhat more tentatively, back to God. Their fingers do not quite touch. What the artist re-creates, however, is a reminder of another thin place: the time when God began creating humanity in God's image and called us good (Genesis 1:31).

These places and stories remind us that God has been reaching out to humanity in many and varied ways across the ages. The biblical stories we have read in this service testify to God reaching to humanity in ways that enrich and transform people's actions and attitudes.

Let us journey, in particular, to a very special "thin" place called Bethlehem in Israel. Mary and Joseph had gone there for the Roman census and to pay their taxes. No room could be found in any guest quarters, and Mary's baby was about to be born. Being offered a stable with straw to lie in, Mary gave birth to her son, wrapped him in bands of cloth, and laid him in a feed trough. Nothing could be remotely considered home in that place. No comfortable reassurances of family or friends were to be found. No trusted persons were there to care for the exhausted mother, father, and their newborn infant, whom they named Jesus.

In the naked vulnerability of the baby Jesus, God entered the world in the flesh. God came to be with us. For centuries God had been searching for ways to reach humanity and build a lasting covenant of love. God had tried the Law, various prophets, priests, and kings. Nothing worked to God's satisfaction. People continued to wander aimlessly, living lives filled with activity but little purpose. Perhaps they would sympathize with our plight of having much to do but little of it having significance.

Into this setting, God stepped. Did you notice who announced this auspicious initiative of God? The royalty and doctors of the Law, as recorded by Matthew, were surprised and terrified when they learned of the event some time later (Matthew 2:3). The ones we might have expected to hear first, in fact, were the last to know.

The ones who were told first were the least, the last, and the lost of society. The beloved Son of God had his humble birth announced by angels to a group of shepherds who were tending their flocks of sheep outside of Bethlehem. Ironically, shepherds were held in such ill repute that their testimony was not allowed in a court of law. They were viewed as social outcasts, scoundrels, liars, and cheats. God chose to give those whom society declared as having nothing worthwhile to say the greatest news ever heard by human ears.

Through the angels God told them:

> *"Do not be afraid; for see — I am bringing you good news of great joy for all the people: to you is born this day in the city of David a Savior, who is the Messiah, the Lord. This will be a sign for you: you will find a child wrapped in bands of cloth and lying in a manger." And suddenly there was with the angel a multitude of the heavenly host, praising God and saying, "Glory to God in the highest heaven, and on earth peace among those whom he favors."*
>
> (Luke 2:10-14)

The shepherds were *humbly awed* at first with the appearance of the angels. As with Mary and Joseph before them, often the first emotion when God reaches out in startling ways or ways that are unusual to us is to feel humbled and afraid. But the assurance of the angels, together with the hope which the good news promised, overcame their fear. The shepherds' perspective began to shift. Their awe turned to an *excited openness*.

Furthermore, their excited openness was followed by a strong, *willing obedience*. The shepherds did not go back to business as usual. They did not consider that few would listen to them. Having been visited by God in this "thin" place, they went to find out more. They said to one another:

> *"Let us go now to Bethlehem to see this thing that has taken place, which the Lord has made known to us." So they went with haste and found Mary and Joseph, and the child lying in the manger.*
>
> (Luke 2:15-16)

The obedience of the shepherds was rewarded. They searched the village and they found the holy family. Luke reports:

> *When they saw this, they made known what had been told them about this child; and all who heard it were amazed at what the shepherds told them. But Mary treasured all these words and pondered them in her heart.*
>
> (Luke 2:17-19)

The good news they had been given not only had an effect on the shepherds, it affected all those who heard their testimony. Even though some may have questioned or doubted, this news was not to be dismissed casually.

In addition to an attitude of *excited openness,* and a *willing obedience*, these simple people, having been touched by God, were characterized by *abundant rejoicing*. "The shepherds returned, glorifying and praising God for all they had heard and seen, as it had been told them" (Luke 2:20).

We find a similar attitude present with the wise men who came to worship Jesus. They saw a star in the East. This sign was used by God to create the opportunity for another "thin" place. The phenomenon gave birth to an *excited openness*. They acted on their openness and planned a costly and dangerous journey across the desert in search of the newborn king of the Jews. This attitude of *willing obedience* to search out the meaning and significance of God's surprising activity led, at last, to Bethlehem. The Gospel of Matthew says, "When they saw that the star had stopped, they were *overwhelmed with joy*. On entering the house, they saw the child with Mary his mother; and they knelt down and paid him homage" (see Matthew 2:1-12). *Abundant rejoicing* is frequently the fruit of excited openness and willing obedience.

I have shared these stories because I wanted us to see afresh, with clarity, with sharp definition, that God has been at work across thousands of years, helping various people come to know and experience His presence in their lives. God is not playing hide and seek with humanity. God is not playing a game of being hard to get with us. Instead, God has been at work in both ordinary and extraordinary events of life, creating "thin" places where we could encounter God in real, powerful, transformational ways. (Cite some "thin place" experiences in the life of the congregation and/or your own life.)

One of the wonderful and profound ways God in Christ reaches out to us is in the sacrament of Holy Communion. This sacrament represents the gift of Jesus' body and blood given for us. His body was broken to make us whole. His blood was poured out to fill our emptiness. The love of God in Christ was manifest in the gift of his life as well as in the gift of his death and resurrection. As we partake this evening, let us give thanks and draw strength from this sacrament to respond to God anew.

Let us pray. Dear God, thank you for creating "thin" places from the beginning of creation until now. Praise you for reaching out to us where we are and lifting us into your presence. Help us through your presence and power to find freedom to resist and overcome the "too much syndrome." In the quietness, we name those things that have received too much of our time, attention, and energy *(pause)*. Grant us grace to enter into the holy, joyous liberty and balance which you desire for our lives. We ask, Lord, that this Christmas you would create within us a humble awe, an excited openness, a willing obedience, and an abundant rejoicing, such as that which characterized the ones who came to pay homage to the Christ Child. Touch us this hour, we pray, and transform this house of worship into a "thin" place. In Jesus' name, we offer our prayer. Amen.

First Sunday In Christmastide

Introduction to this Service:

Everyone is to bring **an evergreen branch** to worship. Extra boughs may be brought by church members and handed out to those who do not have any.

The evergreen is a useful symbol for the Christian life. The focus of the message is to consider how we can remain "evergreen" and fruitful as people of faith.

During enjoyable holiday periods, most of us are like the fresh-cut evergreen. The sweet aroma of our lives is readily lavished on everyone. After these periods of celebration, however, we are faced once again with the mundane round of events in life. This can rob us of our reverie.

How do we maintain a "greenness" that is fresh, vital, and life-enhancing? How do we live a life that is saturated with and sustained by joy? Jesus gave us a clue when he said, "Abide in me...." If we hope to be fruitful, ever-green Christians, we must learn to remain in Christ hour by hour, day by day.

The message prompts people to consider how fruitful and faithful they are being for Christ. Questions are raised to help people think about which spiritual disciplines may help them to abide in Christ more effectively.

CELEBRATING THE LORD'S DAY
FIRST SUNDAY IN CHRISTMASTIDE

OPENING SENTENCE John 15:5

"I am the vine, you are the branches. Those who abide in me and I in them bear much fruit, because apart from me you can do nothing."

PRELUDE "Prelude on 'Morning Star' "

PARISH ANNOUNCEMENTS

*WELCOMING ONE ANOTHER

Shake hands with those around you. Introduce yourself to those you do not know by name. Please remain standing for the "Gathering."

*GATHERING "O Come, Let Us Adore Him"

CALL TO WORSHIP[1]

Leader: We come together from many different places; but we are a part of each other, because we all belong to Christ.

People: We are like many branches of one vine; and Christ is that vine, uniting us to himself.

Leader: We are united to Christ so that he may work through us to bear fruit in his kingdom.

People: We pray that many persons will be brought into God's kingdom of love because of our relationship with Christ.

HYMN "Love Came Down at Christmas"
Trad. Puerto Rican carol

CHILDREN'S MESSAGE

GIVING OF TITHES AND OFFERING

OFFERTORY ANTHEM "Redeeming Love"
William J. Gaither

PRAYER OF CONFESSION[2]

Dear Father, we are followers of your Son, Jesus; but much of our following is often from a distance. And so our discipleship does not bear fruit. Forgive us when we have been satisfied with appearing to be Christian, without bearing the fruit of Christian discipleship. Unite us to Christ in a strong bond of love and loyalty, that the fruit of our labors may bring glory to you. We pray through Christ our Lord. Amen.

PRAYER SONGS

"Create in Me a Clean Heart" Author Unknown
"Change My Heart, O God" Eddie Espinoza
"Purify My Heart" Jeff Nelson

MORNING PRAYER and LORD'S PRAYER

ANTHEM

*GOSPEL LESSON John 15:1-11

Leader: This is the Gospel of our Lord.
People: Praise be to you, Lord Jesus Christ. Amen.

*HYMN "O Christmas Tree"

MORNING MESSAGE "Remaining Ever-Green"

*HYMN "I Need Thee Every Hour"
Annie S. Hawks

*BLESSING

Let us go forth to be ever-green for God. May we continue to abide in Christ that your life and mine will be fruitful and faithful. May Christ's joy be in you and may your joy be full. Amen.

*BLESSING ONE ANOTHER and POSTLUDE

*All who are able please stand

John 15:1-11

Remaining Ever-Green

Please take out the evergreen branch that I asked you to bring with you to church. If you do not have a branch, then look at the one nearest you. Notice the needles. How do they look? They are probably healthy-looking and shiny if you just pruned it off a bush or tree. If you have had the branch out of the water for a time, however, the needles may be starting to show signs of lack of water.

Take a few needles off the branch. Please share some of your needles with those who do not have any. How do the needles feel to the touch? When you bend them, do they flex easily or do they break in two? Obviously, the longer these branches and their needles have been cut off from the tree, the drier they will be and the more susceptible to breaking. If you kept it around until the heat of the summer, the needles would fall off just by touching them.

When the Christmas tree or evergreen branch is freshly cut, it smells wonderful. The aroma of the evergreen fills the air and reminds us of an old-fashioned, traditional Christmas celebration. Fresh-cut trees always take a lot of water, sometimes several quarts a day. They thirstily drink to provide moisture and nutrition for the cells in the trunk, bark, branches, and needles.

Starting immediately after it is cut, and throughout the week following the cutting of an evergreen tree, the trunk and any broken branches secrete a thick, sticky resin called pitch which seals the cut, so as to heal itself and preserve the life-enhancing fluid and food inside the tree. If you've ever had a live Christmas tree you know how sticky this resin is. It is nearly impossible to wash off. You have to remove it with turpentine or paint thinner.

The evergreen is a useful symbol for the Christian life. Let us think together today about how we can remain ever-green as people of faith.

Feeling happy and enthusiastic is not hard for many of us during the holidays and times of celebration. Oftentimes, we have had a few days off. We have broken with the regular routine of life. Special foods have delighted us. Colorful decorations adorn our homes. We are surrounded by family and friends. People have remembered us with cards or gifts. Mutual appreciation and affirmation usually flow more freely in times like this.

During these periods, we are like the fresh-cut evergreen. The sweet aroma of our lives is lavished on everyone. Joy is not only something we yearn for, but also something we feel, if we are capable of it. Prayers are said with a deeper sense of meaning and thanksgiving. God sometimes seems closer and more directly accessible.

What comes after these periods of celebration? The routine. Reality. The mundane round of life begins again. The bills come due. The doctor has to be seen for that postponed test. The diet is resumed. School and jobs call for time and attention. We must put away the decorations. All this threatens to rob us of our reverie. We find that our circumstances, which only a short time before were uplifting and favorable, are now not nearly as enticing.

Is there any alternative to following this roller coaster of highs and lows? How do we maintain a "greenness" that is fresh, vital, and life-enhancing? How do we move beyond living for the weekends, the next vacation, the next holiday? How do we live a life that is saturated with and sustained by joy?

Jesus, speaking in the Gospel of John chapter fifteen, gives us some useful instruction in this regard. As a teacher Jesus used all kinds of object lessons and stories to communicate with people. In this case, he spoke about grapevines. He said, "I am the true vine, and my Father is the vinegrower. He removes every branch in me that bears no fruit. Every branch that bears fruit he prunes to make it bear more fruit" (John 15:1-2).

Jesus likens himself to a vine that God has planted and is tending. The followers of Jesus are likened to branches on the vine. When I read, did you hear what happens to the branches of Jesus' vine? Every branch gets cut for one reason or another. Some branches are cut because they bear no fruit. Other branches are cut because they are bearing fruit and the vinegrower wants to help the branches to produce even better, sweeter, more abundant fruit.

Perhaps you have encountered the attitude on the part of a few church members who believe that they are fulfilling their Christian duty in life simply by showing up on Sunday morning. These people may contribute their presence on occasion but feel little sense of obligation to contribute a significant portion of their time, their talents, or their treasure to God's work. Sadly, these people are like fruitless branches. They are not fulfilling their intended purpose. They are taking more than they are giving. They are using up the resources and energy of the church but making little contribution back to it. Over time this type of people will wither. Their life will turn from "green" to "brown" because they have not fulfilled what God intended for them. They may still come to church, but what happens on Sunday morning will have little carry-over value to the rest of their week. They are going through some of the motions of being Christian, but no vitality or power is visible in their lives. They are like tired, worn-out evergreen boughs that have been cut off from the tree. They may even remind us of the branches of an artificial Christmas tree that have seen better days. They lack the look and feel of authenticity.

Have you ever felt this way? Have you ever wondered if you were truly authentic, fruitful, faithful? Have you felt guilty about taking more than you were giving? While this may be the case for any one of us while going through a severe time of difficulty, such as a death, a divorce, a job change, or a hard pregnancy, we will not make this a pattern for our lives if we want to remain spiritually healthy. Healthy Christians unite together and depend upon Christ and one another as they work to develop a healthy church.

A healthy church is a "Christian producing" church, just as a healthy vine is a grape producing vine. Jesus intends each Christian to be a positive, fruit producing branch in his vine. He wants the "sap" of the Spirit flowing through us promoting growth and close fellowship of the community of faith and acting like pitch to protect the life and heal the wounds of those who are hurting.

Jesus spoke about pruning as essential to any healthy, fruit producing process. In order to maximize the fruit bearing potential of a vineyard, the grower prunes the plant down to a few main vines. All the energy of the plant then goes into these vines and into producing fruit rather than producing more leaves.

In like manner, God prunes us through the inspiration and instruction of the Bible, the wise counsel and correction of caring Christians and the Holy Spirit who convicts us of sin, righteousness, and judgment (John 16:8-11). God prunes us in order that the greatest part of our energy goes into making good fruit. By fruit, I mean the fruits of the Spirit which Saint Paul refers to in his letter to the church at Galatia — love, joy, peace, patience, kindness, generosity, faithfulness, gentleness, and self-control (Galatians 5:22-23).

Christians who are growing in faith, who are learning more about what it means to serve Christ and serve others using their gifts, those who bear witness to their faith in word and deed, those with a sense of God's purpose and call in their hearts, these persons are the kind God wants to produce. They are warm, winsome, and attractive. You can tell by being around them for only a short time that they have an authentic, maturing faith.

How do people become like this? How do *we* become this kind of ever-green Christian? Jesus gave the following instructions. He said:

> *Abide in me as I abide in you. Just as the branch cannot bear fruit by itself unless it abides in the vine, neither can you unless you abide in me. I am the vine, you are the branches. Those who abide in me and I in them bear much fruit, because apart from me you can do nothing ... If you abide in me, and my words abide in you, ask for whatever you wish, and it will be done for you. My Father is glorified by this, that you bear much fruit and become my disciples. As the Father has loved me, so I have loved you; abide in my love ... I have said these things to you so that my joy may be in you, and that your joy may be complete.*
>
> (John 15:4-5, 7-9, 11)

The key word here is "abide." "Abide" means "to remain in," "to continue," "to dwell" in Christ.[3] If we hope to be fruitful, ever-green Christians, we must learn to remain in Christ day by day. A week to week, Sunday to Sunday experience of faith will never sustain us. Just as eating once a week, even if we stuff ourselves, can never be healthy, so also partaking of the truth and power of God on a weekly instead of daily basis will weaken our faith. We will begin to wither. We will dry up and become brittle, just like the evergreen bough when it is severed from the tree.

If we do abide in Christ, however, he promises that we will be fruitful. We will make a difference in our world. Jesus said, "Those who abide in me and I in them bear much fruit" (John 15:5). Jesus also reminds us in this same passage that "apart from him, we can do nothing." Both abiding and fruit bearing are impossible without Christ. We must be rooted, grounded, and well-established in Christ in order to live fully the life God intends.

What is it that you need to do in order to abide more fully in Christ? What do you need to become an ever-green Christian? As you ponder this, let me suggest some specific areas for your consideration. Have you accepted Jesus Christ as your Savior and Lord/Leader? Have you turned to him for cleansing and forgiveness of your sin? How is your daily Bible reading and prayer? What kinds of studies have you been in lately that have enhanced your faith? Is there room for and a desire for improvement in your worship attendance and participation in the life of the church? Where are you serving the Lord, using the unique gifts he has given you? Are you giving a tithe, ten percent of your income, to the work of the Lord as a tangible way of placing your whole trust in God's provision for your life?

The answers to these questions have significant implications for our abiding in Christ and the fruitfulness of our Christian faith. They are asked to prompt us to think about where we are and the ways in which we might grow in order to be more balanced, ever-green disciples. Jesus said, "My Father is glorified by this, that you bear much fruit and become my disciples" (John 15:8). God's intent is that we bear fruit worthy of Christ. In so doing, we will have great joy. This is promised to us by Christ himself in John

15:11. "I have said these things to you so that my joy may be in you, and that your joy may be complete." May the Lord help us to be faithful, fruitful, ever-green Christians as we learn to abide in his presence and grace. Amen.

Let us pray. Lord Jesus, thank you that you want us to abide in you. What a privilege! What a joy! Praise you that you can and will use people like us to build your glorious, everlasting kingdom. Teach us how to abide in you, Lord. Teach us to trust in you, to be patient, to be fruitful. May your kingdom come, and your will be done in us, in our church, in our community, and beyond. We ask these things in the name and spirit of Christ, who makes life purposeful, powerful, joyful, and ever-green. Amen.

---

1. Corl, Heth H. *Lectionary Worship Aids: Revised for Use with the Common Consensus Lectionary, Series B.* Lima, OH: CSS Publishing, 1984, p. 114. Used with permission.

2. *Ibid.* Used with permission.

3. Vine, W. E., Merrill F. Unger, and William White, Jr. *Vine's Complete Expository Dictionary of Old and New Testament Words.* Nashville, TN: Thomas Nelson Publishers, 1985, pp. 1-2.

Second Sunday In Christmastide

Introduction to this Service:

Everyone is to come to church prepared to dedicate to God some portion of their time, talent, and financial resources for use in being a disciple and making disciples of Jesus Christ. This may include serving the church or volunteering in the community. Each commitment will be made before God in a time of dedication at the altar following the message. Families and friends are encouraged to share their commitments with one another in order to pray for one another and support each other in taking these new steps of faith. The goal is to help people think about their disciplemaking responsibilities and begin to take intentional steps to putting their abilities to work for God.

Part of the message uses the image of a triangle and labels each side. You may want to put a triangle on the bulletin cover or make it an insert as an aid to following along and listening to the message.

Please note that at the end of the message, time is given to fill out a commitment card. The format for this card can be found at the conclusion of this chapter. Permission is granted to replicate this form for use in the local church. Enough copies should be made for everyone to have one. If you use a bulletin, I suggest that you make this card an insert.

CELEBRATING THE LORD'S DAY
SECOND SUNDAY IN CHRISTMASTIDE

OPENING SENTENCE Matthew 28:19-20

"Go therefore and make disciples of all nations, baptizing them in the name of the Father and of the Son and of the Holy Spirit, and teaching them to obey everything that I have commanded you."

PRELUDE "Guide Me, O Thou Great Jehovah/Allegro"
arr. by Linda McKechnie

PARISH ANNOUNCEMENTS

*WELCOMING ONE ANOTHER

Shake hands with those around you. Introduce yourself to those you do not know by name. Please remain standing for the "Gathering."

*GATHERING Shine, Jesus, Shine"
Graham Kendrick

*INVOCATION (Unison)

Ever living, ever loving God, you call all of us to be disciples and to make disciples of your Son, Jesus Christ: increase our love which we express through proclamation, service, and Christian fellowship, that your church may effectively live the Gospel with all persons. In our Savior's name we pray. Amen.

*HYMN "Go Tell It On the Mountain"
John W. Work, Jr.

CHILDREN'S MESSAGE

GIVING OF TITHES AND OFFERING

OFFERTORY ANTHEM "Send the Light"
arr. by Humphrey Turner

PRAYER OF CONFESSION (Unison)

Gracious and forgiving God, in this Christmas Season we are called to celebrate the gift of your Son, Jesus Christ. We need to clear away the clutter of things and events that distract us from this great honor and duty. We need to take time to re-center ourselves in you. We need to be empowered to be disciples of Christ. As we commit ourselves this day to be more faithful caretakers of all the gifts you have entrusted to us, help us to focus on ways we can make disciples and thereby honor and glorify you. We pray in the name of Jesus Christ. Amen.

PRAYER SONGS

"The Servant Song" Richard Gillard
"Change My Heart, O God" Eddie Espinoza
"Purify My Heart" Jeff Nelson

MORNING PRAYER and LORD'S PRAYER

ANTHEM

NEW TESTAMENT LESSON Acts 2:37-42

Leader: This is the Word of the Lord.
People: Thanks be to God. Amen.

*GOSPEL LESSON Matthew 28:18-20

Leader: This is the Gospel of our Lord.
People: Praise be to you, Lord Jesus Christ. Amen.

*HYMN "Go, Make of All Disciples"
Leon M. Adkins

MORNING MESSAGE "The Triangle Of Faithful Discipleship"

TIME OF COMMITMENT AT THE ALTAR

*HYMN "Here I Am, Lord"
Dan Schulte

*BLESSING

Go forth to serve God with all that you have and all that you are. Do not neglect the gifts God has entrusted to you. You are blessed and sent forth to be a disciple and to make disciples of Jesus Christ. Amen.

*BLESSING ONE ANOTHER and POSTLUDE

*All who are able please stand

Matthew 28:18-20; Acts 2:37-42

The Triangle Of Faithful Discipleship

Do you feel run down? Does it seem as if there is always something waiting for your attention; no sooner than you get one thing done, another commitment presents itself? Many of us feel harried by our schedules and obligations, especially through the period of the Christmas holidays. We are involved in lots of activities. Most of us manage to use fully every 24-hour day given to us. Sometimes we wish that we just had a little more time. If we had more time in a day, however, we would probably fill that up, too.

More time is not the core issue. The fundamental question is: Are we doing what God wants with our time? Are we using the gifts of our time, talent, and resources in ways that God has directed? Do we have a sense of calling to the positions, places, and people in whom we are investing ourselves? Are the commitments we have made bearing good fruit for God? What changes might we need to make in order to be more faithful?

These questions deserve careful consideration as we assess where we are headed and to what we will make commitments in the new year. We are called to be good stewards and trustees of the gifts God has given us. The Master (Jesus Christ) will one day return and ask us to give an account of what we have done with our responsibilities (Matthew 25:45-51).

Once we have spent our resources, typically we do not have them to use again. This is certainly the case with time, money, and energy. Because these resources need to be replenished over and over, we cannot take them for granted. We are to use them in a manner that glorifies God and serves others.

Jesus modeled faithful stewardship for us. Jesus was intentional about using his time, energy, and resources for God and others. He took time to speak with and listen to God. He sought in all things to be obedient to God, regardless of the cost. For example, after his baptism by John, the Spirit led Jesus into the wilderness where he fasted and prayed for forty days. During this time he was severely tempted by the devil. He overcame each temptation, not in his own power, but by the power of God and the authority of God's Word (Luke 4:1-15). Jesus remained faithful and did not use his gifts to satisfy his physical and material needs, to gain power for himself, or to bring undue attention to himself. He used his gifts to be a servant of God and to disciple other people.

When Jesus had a sense that he needed to train others to be his followers, he prayed all night for God to lead and make clear whom he should ask (Luke 6:12-16). Considering how many times they let him down, we may wonder at times if Jesus made the right choices. Nevertheless, Jesus chose imperfect people, with whom we can identify, to accomplish God's perfect will on earth. This is good news for us. God chooses to work through imperfect, earthen vessels to accomplish his perfect will (2 Corinthians 4:7).

The challenge for Christians is to learn to be faithful with what God has given us. We want to glorify God with what we have and who we are. We want God to be honored through the use of all our resources. We want to be worthy of the wonderful trust God has placed in us.

One way we can be assured that we are doing the will of God is to follow Jesus' instructions. After Jesus was resurrected from the dead and before he ascended into heaven, he told the disciples to wait for the Holy Spirit to come upon them. The Spirit would give them the power they needed to be faithful witnesses, assisting them to use their time, talents, and resources for God's glory.

As I mentioned last Sunday, we were to come to church this week prepared to dedicate to God some portion of our time, talent, and financial resources for use in being more faithful disciples and in making disciples of Jesus Christ. Even if you were not here last Sunday, you do not need to feel awkward or unprepared. We will all be thinking about and making our commitments in the context of worship this morning. Our commitment may include serving the church or volunteering in the community. Each one's commitment will be personal, between you and God. Every commitment will be made asking for God to help us fulfill it. None of us can honor our commitments on a week to week basis without the Lord's strength and power. Families and friends are encouraged to share these personal commitments in order to pray for one another and support each other in taking these new steps of faith. The goal is to help people think about their disciplemaking responsibilities and begin to take the intentional steps of putting their gifts to work for God.

At the conclusion of the message, you and I will have the opportunity to come before God at the altar rail. We will come to renew our relationship with God. We will come to offer to God the gift of ourselves — what we have and what we are. Everyone is encouraged to make a personal commitment to perform some kind of service that will aid others. We will ask God to give us a sense of what we need to do and who God wants to bless through us.

Offering ourselves afresh to the Lord is a great joy. Spiritual strength is released in taking these action steps. During this time, I encourage you to ask God to take control of your time, energy, and financial resources. Ask how you can use these gifts to glorify God and serve others.

Most of us experience our greatest satisfaction when we can give something as well as receive something, when our contributions and our talents can make a significant impact. The happiest, most faithful Christians I know are those who are doing something for Christ and for others. They have goals. Several of them have personal mission statements which guide their lives. They are not living haphazardly but intentionally, prayerfully, faithfully. They are making a difference in others, oftentimes beyond their immediate family responsibilities. They are living as disciples of Christ in the workplace as well as on Sunday mornings.

I heard a church leader once say, "It is relatively easy for me to be a Christian on Sunday mornings. I don't have any pressures here. I have only a few responsibilities. I can come to church, listen to the message, go to Sunday School, and return home. My trouble, in being a faithful Christian, starts on Monday morning and continues throughout the week." Does this sound familiar? Of course it does. If we have any depth and integrity of faith, you and I will struggle with how to be disciples and how to make disciples of Christ every day of the week.

According to the Gospel of Matthew, the primary work of the church is disciplemaking. We become healthy disciples and make disciples in three interrelated ways. I will use a word picture to help you remember my points. Picture in your mind or draw on a piece of paper a triangle. On one side of the triangle, write the word **"proclamation."** The church equips people to be and to make disciples of Jesus Christ by proclaiming the Good News of the Bible: that God was in Christ, not counting our sins and trespasses against us, but offering us forgiveness and reconciliation. Having received this news by faith, and believed in Christ as our Savior from sin and Leader of our life, we are to share him with others. Christ has no other voice but your voice and mine. If we remain silent about our faith in Christ, how are others going to hear? God may want to use you in proclaiming Christ in your workplace, with your children, your spouse, a special friend, or with neighbors.

One of the major needs of our day is for churches and church members to recover their voice. In too many cases we have forgotten and/or neglected the call to offer a verbal witness to the Gospel of Jesus Christ. I have often heard the comment, "We do not want to offend people with our faith." Please listen carefully as I respond to this concern. While I understand and sympathize with the sentiment behind these words, **I strongly believe that it is an offense not to share the Gospel with those we love and for whom we care**. We have great news to share with people! **Are we not offending God and others when we withhold the news of God's love revealed to all humanity in Jesus Christ?** It is a marvelous privilege, rather than an offense, to assist people to take steps toward faith in Jesus Christ for the forgiveness of their sin and the promise of eternal life.

Let us now move to the second side of the triangle. The church's job, and our job as disciples of Christ, is more than being a mouthpiece or a spokesperson. People quickly get impatient when someone is all talk and no action. In light of this, put the word "**service**" on the second side of the triangle. Service is what we *do* with our God-given gifts. Some people are gifted to call on persons in the hospital and the nursing home, or on persons visiting the church. Others are gifted to be greeters at the door Sunday morning or to pass out bulletins in a warm and friendly manner. Still others are gifted musically or are equipped to teach. Some lead meetings well and help us to conduct business effectively. Others are good at keeping track of money and paying the bills. Some people mow lawns, plow snow, paint walls, clean windows, prepare meals, send cards, make phone calls, get mailings ready, and work in the office. Some go on mission trips and assist those in crisis to rebuild their lives. Others give generously to meet the needs of the deprived, support the education of the young, and quietly offer financial help to those who are struggling. These examples are just a few of the items that comprise the service dimension of the church. What has God given you the ability to do? To what types of service are you drawn?

Once we have heard the proclamation of the Scriptures, we need to act upon what we have heard. If we just go home and forget what was said, we are not doing God, ourselves, or the world much good. **Proclamation always requires a response, an outlet, in some form of service.**

The following illustration is an apt parable for the church. Two so-called seas exist in Israel. The one is the Sea of Galilee and the other is the Dead Sea. The Sea of Galilee is alive, refreshing, inviting. Fish abound in its waters. A lush carpet of grass and trees line the slopes of its shores. Commerce and farming abound in the area surrounding Galilee.

The Dead Sea, on the other hand, is appropriately named. Its shores are barren, the atmosphere is harsh, and its bitter water cannot sustain life nor quench thirst.

Why is one sea alive and the other dead? The difference is in the giving. The Sea of Galilee is alive because it has an inlet and an outlet. It takes in life from the Jordan River and it passes on life. The Dead Sea, by contrast, has an inlet but no outlet. It too receives life from the fresh water of the Jordan River, but does not pass on life. All the minerals halt their flow within its boundaries.

In the church, proclamation offers the opportunity for us to take life in. We hear and receive the good news of the Gospel. But we must also have an outlet. We must have "service" to be healthy and whole. If we are coming on Sunday morning only to receive, and are resistant to using our time, talents, and resources for God's glory and to help others to be disciples, we are going to be spiritually dead.

Moving to the third side of the triangle, add the word **"fellowship."** It is wonderful to both *hear* the proclamation and *be* proclaimers of God's Word ourselves. It is tremendous to feel like we are making a difference through the use of our gifts as we seek to be servants of God and others. However, we need fellowship to sustain us. Most of us know Christians who have started out well but have not finished well. One of the recurring reasons for this is the lack of supportive Christian fellowship. We need a group of persons whom we can trust and with whom we can be authentic.

Isolation is detrimental to the Christian life. When we get out of fellowship, we start to wither spiritually. We dry up. We lose our vitality, perspective, and ability to persevere. Christians who are out of fellowship are like fish out of water or like worms on asphalt in the sun. We are unable to survive for very long.

When I see people beginning to miss church, Sunday School, and/or small group experiences, I become concerned. People who could be involved each week but elect to do something else one or more Sundays a month are inviting problems. They will not be spiritually healthy very long. At the very minimum, they will become empty. Eventually, they may have the form of Christianity but not the power of Christ's Spirit flowing through them (2 Timothy 3:5). They will go through the motions of being Christian but they will lack the powerful enthusiasm of contagious Christianity. They will cease to bear the fruit of the Spirit — love, joy, peace, patience, kindness, generosity, faithfulness, gentleness, and self-control (Galatians 5:22-23).

When this happens, we may be able to fool ourselves or others for a while, but Christ is not fooled. In the spiritual realm, we always reap what we sow (Galatians 6:7). Apart from Jesus Christ and fellowship with him and other people of faith, there is no fruit, no abundant life, no joy that is full.

Jesus made this clear in the Gospel of John 15:1-5 to which I referred last week. He said:

> *"I am the true vine, and my Father is the vinegrower. He removes every branch in me that bears no fruit. Every branch that bears fruit he prunes to make it bear more fruit."* [Notice that either way the branch experiences the pain of being cut. We choose our pain. Will our pain be purposeful or meaningless? Will it be pain yielding more fruit or the pain of being cut off altogether?] *Jesus continued, "You have already been cleansed by the word that I have spoken to you. Abide in me as I abide in you. Just as the branch cannot bear fruit by itself unless it abides in the vine, neither can you unless you abide in me."*

The meaning behind the instruction to "abide" in Jesus is the idea of sharing intimate fellowship with him; being open with him; speaking our heart to him without fear of rejection or disapproval. We need to have fellowship like this with Jesus, and we need it with other people of faith.

The life of the early church exemplifies this. The book of Acts says, "They devoted themselves to the apostles' teaching and *fellowship*, to the breaking of bread and the prayers" (Acts 2:42).

Looking more closely at this Acts reference, we find that the early church was characterized by this three-sided ministry. The references to the apostles' teaching, the breaking of bread, and prayers can all be included under the "proclamation" side of triangle. The importance they placed on "fellowship" is clearly evident. They met together in their homes to eat together and to encourage one another, and they went to the temple for worship daily. All this was done in order that their service would be faithful and fruitful. In terms of the "service" dimension of the church, if we read the book of Acts in the New Testament, we find these Christians feeding the hungry, visiting the sick, healing those with infirmities and diseases, driving out demons, proclaiming the Gospel, making disciples of Jesus Christ, and, in general, turning the upside-down world right-side up. It should be no different for the church of Jesus Christ today.

Jesus' parting instructions to his followers were read in the Scriptures this morning. As recorded in the Gospel of Matthew, he told them that they were to make disciples (Matthew 28:18-20). They were to reach out, going wherever people could be found. They were to baptize and teach. In other words, their job was to help people make a commitment to God the Father, Son, and Holy Spirit and then instruct them as to what it meant to be disciples of Jesus Christ. They were to impart to others what they were living every day.

The expectation of Jesus to make disciples is as relevant and essential as it was when it was first given. We are called to proclaim Jesus Christ enthusiastically, to serve willingly using all our time, talents, and resources, and to help to create a contagious fellowship of caring Christians who will be in mission and ministry for Christ in the world.

How are we supposed to undertake all these challenges? We are given the power of the Spirit of God to fulfill the Lord's commands. The book of Acts says that Jesus told his disciples they should wait until the Holy Spirit was given to them. When this happened, they would receive power to be his witnesses in the world (Acts 1:8).

Friends, the work of the church is vitally needed in our day, just as it has been needed in every generation and time. We need to be participants in the dynamic work of being disciples and making disciples through proclamation, fellowship, and service. There are no Christian bystanders in the church of Jesus Christ. We are either out on the playing field, working together as a team, or we are out of the game. What will your commitment be?

Please take out the bulletin insert titled "With God's Help ..." The card reads as follows: I acknowledge God's ownership of everything that I have and accept the responsibility of caring for all that has been entrusted to me. With God's help and in response to the call to be a disciple and to make disciples of Jesus Christ, I dedicate myself to the following:

1) To give _____ hours of my time per week to proclamation, service, and fellowship. I will ask God how and where I can best use this investment of time.

2) To use the following talents to bring honor to God and assistance to others: ____

____.

3) To give a special gift of $____________ beyond my regular offering to show my joy and thanksgiving to God for giving me all that I have and making me all that I am.

Signed ____________________________ Date ____________

In a few moments, I will ask you to complete the card. As you come to the altar rail for a time of prayer and dedication, you are encouraged to ask for God's help in fulfilling this commitment. After you have had time to pray, you will return to your seat by the side aisles. I encourage you to place your card in your Bible or somewhere else where you will look upon it frequently and thus be reminded to pray about fulfilling this commitment with God's help. I also invite you to share your commitment with family members or friends who will support you in this adventure in faith.

We will now pray together before we complete the cards. The ushers will then direct you to come forward for a personal time of dedication and prayer.

Let us pray. Almighty God, we praise you for the church. Thank you for the challenges we face in being and making disciples of Jesus Christ. These challenges cause us to rely on you and not on ourselves. Give to us, once more, the power of your Spirit, that we might boldly proclaim your Word, serve you with love in the world using our gifts, and learn to trust and depend on the encouraging fellowship of other believers. As we come now to this time of commitment, guide us as to what we need to do by way of giving and receiving, that our lives may be more balanced between the three sides of ministry. Lead us as we seek to commit to you afresh our time, talents, and treasure. We pray these things in the name of Jesus Christ our Savior and Lord. Amen.

"With God's Help ..."

I acknowledge God's ownership of everything that I have and accept the responsibility of caring for all that has been entrusted to me. With God's help and in response to the call to be a disciple and to make disciples of Jesus Christ, I dedicate myself to the following:

1) To give _____ hours of my time per week to proclamation, service, and fellowship. I will ask God how and where I can best use this investment of time.

2) To use the following talents to bring honor to God and assistance to others: ____

____.

3) To give a special gift of $________ beyond my regular offering to show my joy and thanksgiving to God for giving me all that I have and making me all that I am.

Signed ___________________________ Date _____________